TOP 25

HOCKEY SKILLS, TIPS, AND TRICKS

E **Enslow Publishers, Inc.**
40 Industrial Road
Box 398
Berkeley Heights, NJ 07922
USA
http://www.enslow.com

JEFF SAVAGE

Library of Congress Cataloging-in-Publication Data

Savage, Jeff, 1961–
   Top 25 hockey skills, tips, and tricks / Jeff Savage.
       p. cm. — (Top 25 sports skills, tips, and tricks)
   Includes index.
   Summary: "Discusses hockey skills, including the proper techniques
for skating, controlling the puck, passing, shooting, and defense and
provides drills, fun tricks, and tips from the pros"—Provided by
publisher.
   ISBN 978-0-7660-3869-1
   1. Hockey—Juvenile literature. I. Title.
   GV847.25.S28 2011
   796.962—dc22

                        2011000286

Paperback ISBN 978-1-59845-357-7

Printed in the United States of America

052011 Lake Book Manufacturing, Inc., Melrose Park, IL

10 9 8 7 6 5 4 3 2 1

Do not attempt the more advanced skills and tricks without adult supervision.

To Our Readers:
We have done our best to make sure all Internet addresses in this book were active and appropriate when we went to press.
However, the author and the publisher have no control over and assume no liability for the material available on those Internet
sites or on other Web sites they may link to. Any comments or suggestions can be sent by e-mail to comments@enslow.com or
to the address on the back cover.

♻ Enslow Publishers, Inc., is committed to printing our books on recycled paper. The paper in every book contains 10% to
30% post-consumer waste (PCW). The cover board on the outside of each book contains 100% PCW. Our goal is to do our part
to help young people and the environment too!

Illustration Credits: AP Images, p. 15; AP Images / Bruce Bisping, p. 45; AP Images / Charles Rex Arbogast, p. 41; AP
Images / Danny Moloshok, p. 30; AP Images / Gene J. Puskar, p. 7 (bottom); AP Images / Gerry Broome, p. 26; AP Images /
J. Meric, p. 21; AP Images / Julio Cortez, p. 39 (top); AP Images / Keith Srakocic, p. 44; AP Images / Luis M. Alvarez, p. 43;
AP Images / Mike Carlson, p. 34; AP Images / Reed Saxon, p. 19; Enslow Publishers, Inc., p. 4; © Joseph Gareri / iStockphoto
.com, p. 39 (bottom); Ken Argent / Frozen Image Photography, pp. 11, 12, 14, 29; © Michael Braun / iStockphoto.com, pp. 23,
31; Shutterstock.com, pp. 1, 7 (top), 9, 13, 17, 18, 22, 25, 33, 37, 40, 42; © technotr / iStockphoto.com, p. 35.

Cover Illustration: Shutterstock.com (Young player passing the puck).

CONTENTS

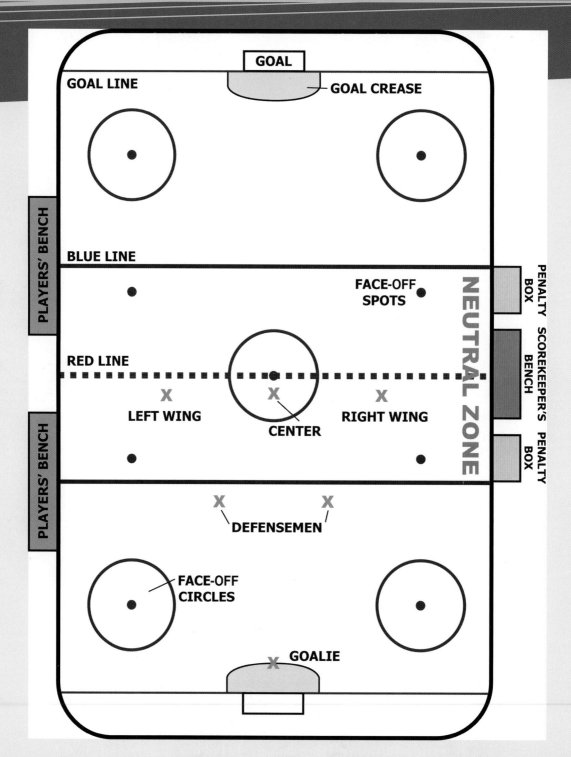

GOAL

GOAL LINE

GOAL CREASE

PLAYERS' BENCH

BLUE LINE

FACE-OFF SPOTS

NEUTRAL ZONE

PENALTY BOX

RED LINE

SCOREKEEPER'S BENCH

X
LEFT WING

X
CENTER

X
RIGHT WING

PENALTY BOX

PLAYERS' BENCH

X   X
DEFENSEMEN

FACE-OFF CIRCLES

X GOALIE

SKATING

Skating is the most important skill in hockey. You might be able to slap a puck or block a shot better than anyone. But if you can't skate, you can't excel at hockey. You must be able to skate in any direction, at different speeds, and, most important, under control.

1 BALANCE

Correct posture is critical to maintaining control on your skates. Your body position will change depending on the direction you go, but there are two general rules you should follow:

1. Keep your weight over your skates.
2. Keep your head up.

When standing or gliding, your skates should be about shoulder-width apart, knees bent, upper body straight, and chest out. Keep your weight on the flat middle of your skates. When skating slowly forward or backward, you should widen your stance so that you are on the inside edges of your skates. Move your weight forward to the balls of your feet. This is called the ready position. When you skate fast, you are on a single skate, shifting from side to side. Be sure to maintain proper posture while shifting your weight over the skate that is on the ice.

2 STARTING AND STRIDING

The key to effective skating is quickness. Sheer speed in a race across the ice is important. But in most situations in hockey, it is the first few steps that make the difference. To beat your opponent to a spot or to get a loose puck first, you need an explosive start.

For a quick burst of speed, your toes should be pointed out with one skate slightly ahead of the other. Dig the edge of your forward skate into the ice, bend your knees, and press your weight over your forward skate. This is your push leg. You are coiled and ready to spring. Push hard off your leg. Launch ahead and quickly bring your rear skate forward just above the ice. Shift your weight toward your glide leg. Fully extend your push leg until the toe is up off the ice and your weight is completely over your glide leg. Your glide leg now becomes your push leg. Repeat the process.

PRO TIPS AND TRICKS

Sidney Crosby is the dynamic player from the Pittsburgh Penguins of the National Hockey League (NHL). Crosby uses tricky moves to escape his opponents. "It's satisfying to break free when they are shadowing you," Crosby says. "You can't afford to go out there and watch too much. If you get caught watching, you're not going to get the puck, and you're not going to make good plays."

Keep your head up.

Shift your weight over the skate that is on the ice.

Bend your knees

Accelerate forward off your push leg.

Glide leg

Your start technique is important because if you can accelerate quicker than your opponent, you will get to the loose puck first. Once you get going, the fastest skaters take the fewest strides. Long, powerful strides will make you a faster skater.

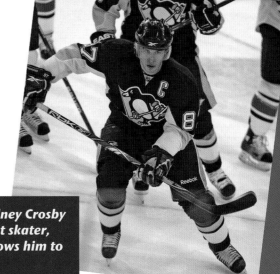

Pittsburgh Penguins center and captain Sidney Crosby is one of the best players in the NHL. A great skater, he is in constant motion on the ice. This allows him to make plays for himself and his teammates.

3 SKATING FAST

Sometimes you need to skate at maximum speed. Avoid the temptation to stand upright. Stay bent at the waist and keep your glide leg bent at the knee to stay low and ready for your next hard push stroke. Extend your back leg as far as possible. Your toe should push off the ice at the last possible instant. To generate more speed, move your arms and shoulders in sync with your legs. For instance, when your right leg moves forward, your right arm and shoulder should swing forward with it. This is the opposite of running, in which your right leg and left upper body move forward together.

You will not always skate in a straight line. To maintain your speed or accelerate in a curve, you want to use the crossover move. That is, you want to cross your outside skate over your inside skate. If you want to curve to your right, with your right knee bent, push off with your left (outside) leg. Lift your left skate and cross it over in front of the toe of your right skate. Push off your right skate and repeat with as many left-skate crossovers as necessary until you are headed in the direction you want to go.

DID YOU KNOW?

Hockey is the fastest team sport. Pro skaters reach speeds up to thirty miles per hour. The puck can travel more than one hundred miles per hour.

Cross your outside skate over your inside skate.

The crossover technique allows a player to accelerate and change direction at the same time. When you crossover to the left, you should be on the outside edge of the left skate and the inside edge of the right skate. The opposite is true for turning right.

4 SKATING BACKWARD

Skating backward looks difficult. But it is easier than you think. Squat as though you are about to sit in a chair. Turn your left foot inward and put most of your weight over that leg. Push off the inside edge of your blade. Straighten your left leg as you turn your foot outward so that it curves on the ice in the shape of the letter C. Transfer your weight over your opposite (right) leg. Be sure the gliding skate of your right leg is aimed in the direction you want to go. Now repeat the movement with your right leg. As you push off again, your right foot should form a backward C. Increase your speed by swinging your hips from side to side in sync with your legs. Skating backward is used especially to defend your opponent. Practice it often.

THEN AND NOW

Hockey got its start on frozen ponds and lakes. It began in Europe more than five hundred years ago. The sport's origin is unclear. It is believed by some to have gotten its name from the French word *hoquet,* which means "shepherd's crook" or "bent stick." The first use of rules came in 1877 when the "Montreal Rules" and the "Halifax Rules" were printed in local Canadian newspapers. Today's game is played mostly on indoor and outdoor rinks. The NHL rink is 200 feet long and 85 feet wide.

Bend at the waist and squat

Increase your speed by rotating your hips in sync with your legs.

Bend your knees and shift your weight over the leg that is carving the C-cut.

Skates carve C-cuts using the inside edge of the blades.

Skating backward is especially important for defense. Offensive players have to react quickly to strong backward skaters.

5 STOPPING

If you skate, at some point you must stop. There are several ways to stop. To stop slowly, use the two-foot snowplow. With your feet wide, turn your toes inward. Scrape the ice with the inside edges of your skates, making sure to keep the blades flat against the ice. Keep your knees bent as you gradually slow to a stop.

The one-foot snowplow is similar, except that you turn the toe of a single skate inward while gliding straight on the other skate. You can also use the two-foot or one-foot snowplow to stop backward. Turn your feet in reverse, so your toes are pointed out. Press the inside edges of your blades into the ice.

To stop more quickly, use the T-stop. Glide on your left skate. Lift your right skate and place it behind and perpendicular to your left skate with your toe pointed outward. Stand straight, lean back slightly, and press down on the outside edge of your back skate while bending at the knee.

To stop abruptly, use the two-bladed stop. This is also called the hockey stop. Turn your entire body and blades sideways. Dig the inside edge of your forward skate and outside edge of your rear skate into the ice. You should send ice chips flying!

Scrape the ice with the inside edge of your blades.

Push your heels out

Point your toes inward

The first stop most hockey players learn is called the snowplow. This type of stop will slow you down gradually.

The hockey stop requires a lot of practice, but it is the best way to stop on a dime. Turn your body and skates sideways. The hockey stop should create a cloud of ice chips.

CONTROLLING THE PUCK

You cannot score in hockey unless you can control the puck. You must be able to gain control of the puck, maintain control, and give and receive passes. Controlling the puck creates scoring opportunities.

 THE GRIP

You want to handle your stick with the correct grip. Your top hand is your control hand. Place your top hand over the knob at the top end of the stick shaft. You should be able to twist the stick in this hand. Your bottom hand is your power hand. Place your bottom hand about twelve inches apart from your top hand. Do not squeeze the stick with the palm of your hand. Instead, grip it mostly with your fingers. Also, your power hand does not need to be the stronger of your two hands. Many players prefer using their dominant hand on the top of their stick for a better sense of control. Lower your bottom hand slightly for passing and even more for shooting. Lower both hands to protect the puck when an opponent is checking you.

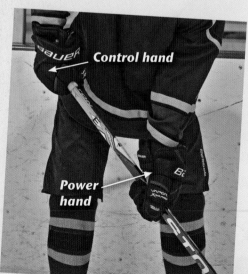

Control hand

Power hand

This is the basic grip of a hockey stick. Your grip will change in different situations, such as protecting and controlling the puck, passing, shooting, or face-offs.

THEN AND NOW

Pro hockey players once played without helmets or pads. Even goalkeepers did not wear any protection. Injuries were common. Goalie John Bower of the NHL's Toronto Maple Leafs lost twenty-eight teeth. Players eventually put safety first. In 1974, Gump Worsley of the Minnesota North Stars was the last NHL goalie to put on a mask. By then, he had 250 stitches in his face. Today, pro hockey players wear nearly thirty pounds of clothing and equipment. Much of it is protective padding.

Pro hockey players did not always wear pads and helmets. Injuries were common and players lost a lot of teeth. Gump Worsley (left, goalie) was the last NHL goalie to play without a mask. In this photo, he plays in a game for the New York Rangers in November 1954.

STICKHANDLING

Stickhandling is simply controlling the puck while skating around opponents. Your stick blade is probably curved. Use the curved side to cup (cover) the puck. Cupping the puck is a great way to protect it from your opponent. But you can't get very far while cupping it. To skate fast with the puck, you need to dribble it. This is done by making tiny, rapid passes to yourself.

The easiest stickhandling technique to master is the side-to-side dribble. Keep the puck out in front of you. Tap the puck from side to side with the middle of your blade. Learn to dribble the puck without watching it.

A harder dribble to learn is the forward-and-back technique. Keep the puck more to your side this time. Using the middle of your blade again, tap the puck forward slightly. Then tap it backward. To dribble farther from your body, use only your top hand.

You don't always have to dribble. When you are in the clear, you can just push the puck ahead of you and skate to it. But be sure not to send it so far ahead that someone else reaches it first.

DID YOU KNOW?

Icing isn't just frosting on a cake. It is a pass or a shot from the defensive half of the rink that crosses over the goal line and is touched first by an opposing player besides the goalie.

Keep your head up so you can see your teammates and opponents.

Keep the puck close to your body to keep it away from defenders.

The top hand is the most important in stickhandling. The top hand can steer the stick blade more quickly than the bottom hand. Great players must be able to control the puck. Jarome Iginla is a great goal scorer for the Calgary Flames. But a superstar goal scorer must also be able to handle the puck.

8 BASIC PASSING

You don't always want to be stickhandling. Hockey is a team sport. Passing to your teammates moves the puck faster than you skating with it. Accuracy is the key. You want to aim your pass in front of your teammate's stick.

The two basic passes are the forehand pass and the backhand pass. The forehand pass is the easiest to do. Start with the puck out in front of you and even with your back foot. Cup, or cradle, the puck in the middle of your blade. Keep both hands away from your body. Sweep your stick forward while keeping your blade flat on the ice and square to the target. Shift your weight from your back foot to your front foot. Follow through and release the puck when it is even with your front foot.

The backhand pass requires the same stick angle and sweep as the forehand pass. However, on a backhander, your body tends to rise. This motion causes your blade to lift and the puck to go into the air. To combat this, keep your lower (forward) shoulder down as you follow through on the pass.

Moving the puck by passing it to your teammates will create more successful scoring opportunities than trying to skate with the puck by yourself. The basic forehand and backhand passes sweep the puck along the ice.

Wayne Gretzky, known as "The Great One," holds the NHL single-season and career records for goals, assists, and points (goals and assists combined). A magician on the ice, Gretzky mastered every type of pass. But like all players, even he started by learning the basic pass.

PRO TIPS AND TRICKS

Wayne Gretzky is considered the greatest hockey player ever. He is the NHL's all-time goals and assists leader. Gretzky says there are two types of passes. "One is solid and hard, and the other is known as the feather," he explains. "If the player you are passing to is standing still, use the firm pass. And if he is going at a good rate of speed, use the feather."

9 FANCY PASSING

Sometimes your opponent is directly in front of you. A basic pass is unlikely to work. This is where you can use a trick pass.

A flip pass works to lift the puck over a defender's stick or body. Start by sweeping the puck forward as you would for a basic forward pass. But instead of following through with your blade flat and square, pull the puck closer toward you by twisting your wrists to get your blade under the puck. Now quickly snap your wrists up and out to flip the puck into the air. Follow through with your hands and blade rising.

Sometimes your path is completely blocked. Even a flip pass won't work. Here you can use a drop pass. For this trick, you don't actually pass the puck. You "leave" it behind for your trailing teammate. To execute the drop pass, simply stop the puck by putting your blade in front of it. Skate away, taking your opponent with you. If you time it right, your teammate skating forward will swoop in and collect the loose puck.

You can pass with more than just your stick. To get out of a tight check, try a nifty skate kick. You can pass the puck to yourself. Or, to get past an opponent along the boards, bounce the puck off the boards at the correct angle. As you skate past your opponent, the puck will return to you.

Martin St. Louis, a right winger for the Tampa Bay Lightning, flips a pass to his teammate. There are many trick passes you can use to move the puck to a teammate when an opponent is blocking your path.

10 RECEIVING A PASS

As in football, a pass in hockey only works if it is "complete." To receive a pass, first you need to get open. If you are being shadowed, use your skating skills to shake free from your opponent. Now give your teammate a target. Keep your stick on the ice. Call out to your teammate, if your coach allows it, or tap your stick on the ice.

Receiving a pass requires touch. If you keep your stick firm, the puck will carom off your blade and bounce away. Soften your grip and pull the blade back slightly as the puck arrives. This allows you to "catch" the puck.

Be ready for any sort of pass. If the pass is far out in front of you, let go of the stick with your bottom hand. Bend your knees and reach out with your top hand. For a pass behind you, reach back one-handed with your stick. You don't have to receive passes only with your stick. You can use your skates. Angle your skate so the pass deflects forward to your stick blade. You can even catch a pass in the air with your hand as long as you drop it immediately.

Not every pass you receive will be perfect. Be ready to reach out for the puck with one hand on your stick. You can also receive passes with your skates. You can catch a pass, too, but you must put the puck down on the ice right away.

Constant motion is essential to getting open for a pass. If you are standing still, your teammate won't be able to get you the puck.

Tap your stick on the ice to let your teammate know you are open.

Keep active and be ready to move the puck once you receive it.

Pull your blade back as the puck arrives to cradle a hard pass.

The object in hockey is to score more goals than your opponent. You can score only if you shoot. There are many ways to shoot. The key is to shoot quickly and accurately.

11 WHERE TO SHOOT

An NHL hockey goal is four feet high and six feet wide. Today's goalkeeper wears oversized leg pads and carries a stick and giant glove. That doesn't leave much space to get the puck past the goalie. It is nice to have a powerful shot, but the goalie can stop any shot that comes straight on. You need to shoot at the five "holes," or small areas, where the goalie is not. Assuming the goalie holds the stick in his right hand, here are the five holes you should shoot for:

1. Low to the goalie's stick side. The "one hole" is the lower left corner and the most difficult hole for the goalie to protect.
2. Low to the goalie's glove side. It is hard to stop low shots anywhere.
3. High to the goalie's stick side. The "three hole" is the upper left corner. It is best for right-handers to shoot backhanded at the "top shelf stick side."
4. High to the goalie's glove side. The upper right corner may seem easy for the goalie to protect by raising his glove, but some goalies hold their glove too low and are slow to react.
5. The "five hole" is directly between the goalie's leg pads.

You will almost always be moving before taking a shot. It's good to practice shooting at the goal from different angles. Also, patience can pay off. The goal may look covered, but the slightest movement by the goalie may create a new "hole" for a shot.

When the goalie stands in goal, there are five "holes" where you can aim your shots.

12 WHEN TO SHOOT

The best time for you to shoot is based on where you are on the ice and what is in front of you. For instance, if you are in the slot, which gives you a good angle in front of the net, and no defenseman is blocking your path—shoot! On the other hand, if you are outside the slot, and a defenseman is checking you, it would be wiser to pass to a teammate who is filling the slot. Don't just whack the puck toward the goal because it seems you are close to it. However, if no teammate is available, and you cannot skate to a better position, you might as well shoot the puck out in front of the net. Who knows? It could get deflected into the goal.

Advanced players lean into their sticks. This creates stick bend, which provides a whipping action and extra power.

Move the lower hand down for more control and power.

Cup the puck between the middle and heel of your blade.

Carolina Hurricanes center Eric Staal fires a wrist shot during training. The wrist shot is the basic forehand hockey shot, and it is considered the most accurate and effective.

13 BASIC SHOTS

More goals are scored on forehand shots than any other. This basic shot is also called a wrist shot. Start with the puck well back in your stance. Slide your lower hand down the stick shaft to increase power and control. Cup the puck between the middle and heel of your stick blade. Sweep your stick forward. Start shifting your weight over your front leg. Keep your stick blade pressed into the ice. At once, pull your upper wrist back and snap your lower wrist forward. Follow through with power. You can skid the puck along the ice by keeping your stick blade low on the follow-through. You can lift the puck into the air by raising your stick blade on the follow-through.

The backhand shot is the reverse of the forehander. A curved stick blade makes this shot more difficult. Keep the puck on the heel of your blade for better control. Sweep your stick, shift your weight, and snap your wrists as you would for a forehander. Drive the puck forward while keeping your front shoulder down during your follow through.

PRO TIPS AND TRICKS

Mark Messier is the only player in NHL history to captain two different teams to the Stanley Cup title. Messier's teams won the cup six times. Messier explains the key to winning control of the puck on a face-off. "Always watch the linesman's hands when the puck is about to be dropped," Messier says. "Forget about the other player. Keep your eyes on the linesman because he's the one who actually has the puck."

14 TRICK SHOTS

There are moments when you don't have time or range for a basic forehand or backhand shot. In these instances, you can use trickier shots. The snap shot is the quickest shot you can take. It is a shortened version of the forehander. The puck can be anywhere on your forehand side, even right next to your skates. Don't take a windup. Simply snap your wrists hard. Twist your body to add power. Keep your knees bent as you follow through. Transfer your weight forward and don't lean back.

The most dramatic shot is the slap shot. It is best used from long range, when you need extra power. It is hard to control, but fun to try. Start with the puck in front of your forward foot. Keep your head down with your eyes locked on the puck. Slide your lower hand down the stick shaft. Grip tight. The motion is similar to a golf swing. Pull your stick back to at least waist height. Swing your arms and shoulders forward and down to put all your strength into it. Strike the ice with your blade about one inch behind the puck. Snap your wrists. Thrust your weight forward. The force of your swing will send the blade into the puck. Follow through and hope for the best!

DID YOU KNOW?

A goal is scored only when the entire puck crosses over the red goal line. Even if most of the puck is across the line, but the back end of it is on the line, it is not a goal.

Bring your stick back above waist level.

Lower your hand for more power.

Snap your wrists bringing all your weight forward with the shot.

Focus on the puck and strike just behind it.

The slap shot is not the most accurate, but if you are shooting from long range it provides extra power.

15 DEFLECTIONS AND SCREENS

Sometimes you can score a goal without taking a shot. By positioning yourself near the goal, you can score on a deflection. An ideal spot to be is on either side of the goal. You can redirect any shot headed wide toward the goal. Take a wide stance for stability and hold your stick firmly on the ice. When a shot comes your way, angle your stick blade so it can deflect the puck toward the goal. You can also score on a rebound from this position. If a shot bounces off the goalie, you will be there to flip the puck into the net.

You can also create a goal without even touching the puck. Do this by screening the goalie. Goalies can't block shots they can't see. You can stand in front of the goalie, as long as you are not in the crease. Stand with your back to the goalie so you can

see the action. But be aware that opponents don't like you trying to block their goalie's vision. Be prepared for body contact!

In hockey, many goals are scored on deflections and rebounds. They may not be the prettiest goals, but they are just as effective. The best place to collect rebounds is in the slot and to the sides of the net. Anticipate where the rebound will go and get there first. But defenders don't like attackers standing in front of their goal. Be ready for physical play.

THEN AND NOW

The first hockey games in North America were played in the 1870s in Canada. Each team had nine players on the ice at once. In the late 1880s, a team showed up for a game with just seven players. Their opponent agreed to play seven-on-seven. The teams preferred having more room to skate. Today, of course, there are six players per side.

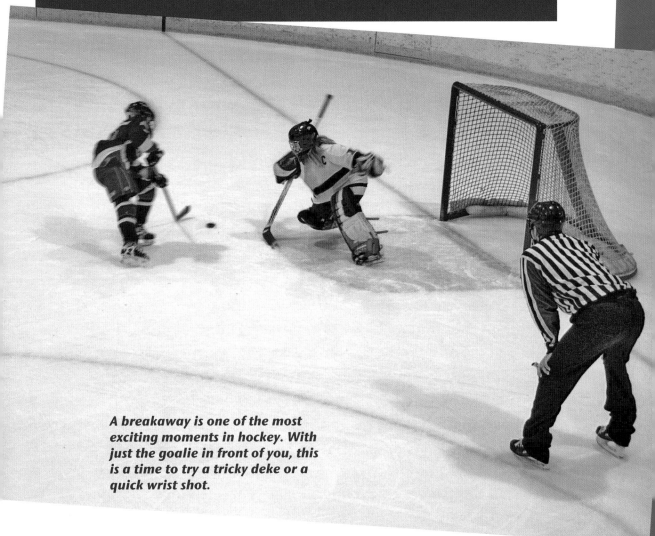

A breakaway is one of the most exciting moments in hockey. With just the goalie in front of you, this is a time to try a tricky deke or a quick wrist shot.

DEFENSE

Scoring goals in hockey is fun. Preventing a goal from being scored is just as important. If the other team does not score, you cannot lose the game. Only two of the six players are called defensemen. However, every player on the ice must play defense.

 # BEING IN POSITION

So much of playing defense is positioning and angling. If you are in the right position, you can force your opponent with the puck to go where you want. On the other hand, if you are out of position, your opponent is free to attack in any direction.

If you are defending an attacker with the puck, you must watch the attacker's chest. Do not watch the puck. Unless the attacker is within range to shoot, skate backward as fast as your opponent moves forward. Maintain a position slightly left or right to force the attacker to go one way—either into the boards or toward one of your defensive teammates. In other words, "overplay" one side.

If you are directly in front of the attacker, he has a choice to skate or pass left or right. But if, for instance, you position yourself at an angle to the right of the attacker, he is forced to go left, where you know you have a teammate ready to help you. This is called funneling. Teamwork is the key here.

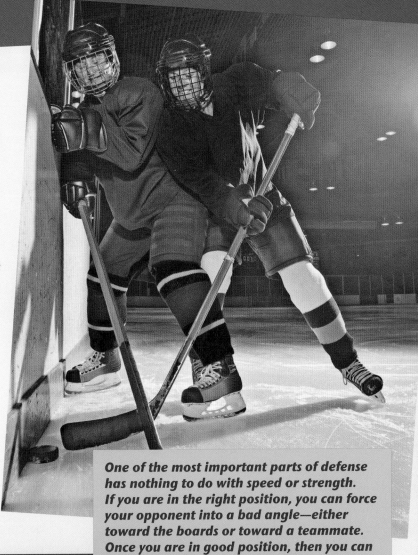

Make sure you have a teammate nearby. One general rule is to force your attacker away from the middle of the ice.

If you are a defenseman, there will be times when you are faced with a two-on-one situation. You should guard the attacker without the puck. Let your goalie focus on the puck carrier. By preventing a pass, you are allowing your goalie to stay in position and focus on just one attacker.

One of the most important parts of defense has nothing to do with speed or strength. If you are in the right position, you can force your opponent into a bad angle—either toward the boards or toward a teammate. Once you are in good position, then you can go after the puck.

THEN AND NOW

The NHL started its first season in 1917 with four teams and finished with three. The Montreal Wanderers quit the league when their arena burned to the ground. Today, there are thirty teams, including two of the original three: the Montreal Canadiens and the Toronto Blueshirts (now called the Maple Leafs).

17 DEFENSIVE TECHNIQUE

You can defend your attacker two ways:

1. By facing him with your back to your goal.
2. By skating alongside him toward your goal.

Facing your attacker is called forechecking. This technique starts as soon as your opponent gains control of the puck. You want to forecheck your attacker starting in your opponent's zone. If you can dislodge the puck and regain possession, you will have the advantage. Do not skate directly at your attacker.

Forecheck at an angle. If your opponent is headed up ice in a rush, defend with a backcheck. Stay with your attacker all the way into your own zone. Stay ahead of your attacker to make him or her less available to receive a pass. Backchecking is easier because you can skate faster forward than backward.

Buffalo Sabres center Derek Roy forechecks Tampa Bay Lightning defenseman Mike Lundin during an NHL game in March 2010. A good defender forechecks at an angle, trying to dislodge the puck and regain possession.

18 STICK CHECKING

If you are forechecking or backchecking the puck carrier, you certainly want to steal the puck. One way to take the puck is with your stick. This is called a stick check. The easiest stick check is the poke check. Hold your stick with just your top hand so you can reach farther. Poke your stick blade at the puck or your attacker's blade. Another effective stick check is called the sweep check. Again, hold your stick with your top hand only. Crouch low and put your stick shaft along the ice. Sweep the shaft in a wide circular motion, as if it were a hand on a clock. Try to knock the puck off your opponent's stick. You can also use the stick lift, in which you lift your attacker's stick blade with yours while stealing the puck with your skate. Finally, you can use the stick press, in which you push down on your attacker's stick blade with yours.

Once you contain the attacker with a forecheck or backcheck, use a stick check to steal the puck away. Keeping only your top hand on the stick, poke your stick at the puck or your opponent's stick.

BODY CONTACT

There are times when you want to stop your attacker by blocking his or her path. Body checking is ramming your body into your opponent. Pros use shoulder checks, hip checks, board checks, and other forms of body checking. The best time to body check is when an opponent is passing or receiving a pass because the opponent is focused on the puck. However, most youth leagues do not allow body checking. If yours does, be sure to keep your elbows down. "Elbowing" is dangerous and a major penalty.

You can still use your body to stop an attacker. A certain amount of contact is allowed. If you are skating alongside your attacker in a backcheck, you can lean in with your upper body to direct your opponent off course. Just don't send him or her into the boards. You can block your attacker's path on a forecheck as long as you are in the lane first. Turn your upper body slightly, bend your knees, and brace yourself. If the attacker cannot stop or change direction in time, a collision will result. Just be sure to play within the rules.

PRO TIPS AND TRICKS

Hall of Fame goaltender Patrick Roy won two Stanley Cup titles with the Montreal Canadiens and two more with the Colorado Avalanche. In 2004, Roy was voted the greatest goaltender in NHL history. Roy preferred the butterfly stance over the stand-up stance. "The butterfly is the position where you cover the most surface of the ice," he says. "I know 60 percent of the goals are scored on the ice. If I can't cover the ice I'm in trouble."

Professional hockey has a lot of body checking and serious collisions. Many youth leagues do not allow body checking. But you can still use your body to frustrate an attacker. In a forecheck or backcheck, lean in on an attacker to direct him or her off course or to block his or her path. Just make sure not to commit a penalty or you will give your opponent a power play.

20 GOALTENDING

Playing goalie in hockey takes courage. You are your team's last line of defense. You want to have a take-charge attitude. Above all, watch the puck!

Choose between two stances. For the stand-up stance, bend at the waist and knees. Keep your leg pads together and point your toes slightly outward to be ready to spring left or right. Keep your stick blade flat on the ice and your catch glove open and low at your side. For the butterfly stance, drop to your knees with your leg pads fanned out to block the lower corners. Raise your hands to block the upper corners.

Use your catch glove when you can. That way, you have control of the puck and can give it to a teammate. If you cannot catch it, block it with your backhand glove, stick, leg pads, or skates. If you can, direct the puck into the corner of the rink. For a leg-pad save, bend your knees a bit just as the puck makes contact. The puck is more likely to drop in front of you where you can sweep it aside or cover it up. Use your stick to make poke checks and sweep checks.

You want to move side to side or in and out to reduce the puck-carrier's angle. Move while maintaining your stance. How far out from the goal should you go? Follow these two rules:

1. Don't stray so far that you cannot get back in the time it takes your opponent to make one extra pass to another onrushing attacker.

2. If the puck is loose out front, and you think you can reach it first—go out and get it!

DID YOU KNOW?

Stopping a shot on goal is called a save. In professional hockey, most goalies stop nine out of every ten shots attempted.

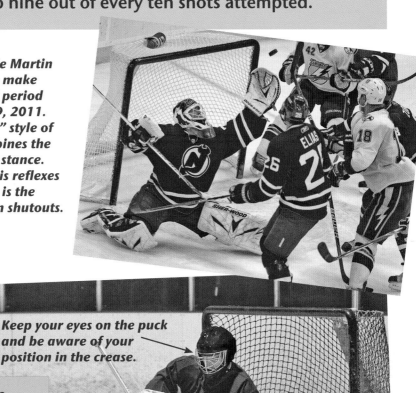

New Jersey Devils goalie Martin Brodeur reaches out to make a save during the third period of a game on January 9, 2011. Brodeur uses a "hybrid" style of goaltending. This combines the butterfly and stand-up stance. Brodeur is known for his reflexes and puck handling. He is the NHL's all-time leader in shutouts.

Keep your eyes on the puck and be aware of your position in the crease.

Catch glove

This goalie makes a save from the butterfly stance. In addition to making saves with their body, stick, and glove, great goalies must be able to cover up rebounds, handle the puck, and distribute the puck to teammates. Anticipation, lateral movement, and good balance are all essential for good goaltending.

Turn knees inward to close the gaps the puck can fit through.

GETTING READY TO PLAY

To play hockey well, you can't just lace up your skates, grab a stick, and go. You need to prepare. Here are some more tips to give you an extra edge.

21 STRETCHING

To protect your body from injury, you must stretch. Stretching helps you get limber and prevents muscles and ligaments from pulling or tearing. Before you stretch, you need to warm up to get your blood flowing. Go on the ice for a few minutes of easy skating. Now you are ready to stretch. First, take a wide stance. Reach down and touch the ground in front of you. Now touch the ground below you. If you can, reach to touch the ground behind you. Next, stand normally. Lift one foot behind you and grab it with your hand. Pull up to stretch the front of your leg. Switch legs. Finally, sit in a chair. Cross one leg over the other with your ankle on your knee. Lean forward. Switch legs.

Hockey is an amazingly fast game. If you're not physically ready to play, it could lead to injury. Make sure to warm up and stretch before practices and games.

THEN AND NOW

In 1892, the governor-general of Canada, Lord Stanley of Preston, awarded a trophy to the top hockey team in Canada. The trophy became known as the Stanley Cup. Each year, the cup is engraved with the names of the winning players, coaches, and staff. Today it weighs nearly thirty-five pounds. The cup is taken to events to promote charity and hockey. Otherwise, it is on display at the Hockey Hall of Fame.

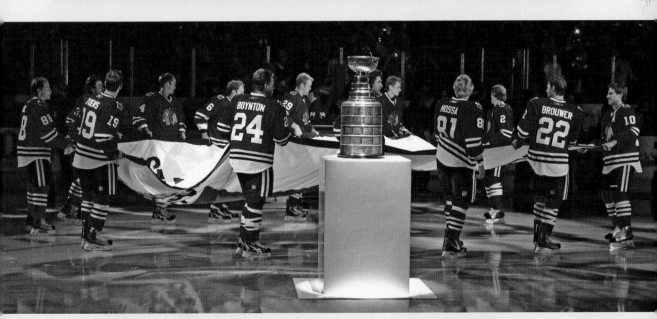

Members of the 2010 Chicago Blackhawks carry the championship banner past the Stanley Cup (center). The Stanley Cup, a trophy first awarded in 1892, is now given to the NHL team that captures the championship each season.

22 NUTRITION

To be an elite athlete, you need to eat properly. You should eat plenty of fruits and vegetables, along with a variety of proteins and whole grains. Two hours or so before the game, you should eat a sandwich or some pasta and a piece of fruit. Between each period you can eat another piece of fruit. You may feel cool on the ice, but your body is certainly warm beneath your uniform and pads. Be sure to drink plenty of water! Skip the snacks until after the game.

When the referee drops the puck at center ice, the game begins. Will you win the face-off? It takes a lot of preparation to play your best. Make sure to eat right, work hard at practice, and take extra time to work on the weaker parts of your game.

23 PRACTICE

Some players goof off in practice. Do not join them. Treat practice as your chance to improve. Listen to your coach. Learn from each drill. Focus every minute, just as you would in a game. If you can, be the first player on the ice and the last to leave. Shoot at the corners of an empty net. If you can't use the net, fire shots at a spot against the boards. Practice at home wherever you can find a slick surface. Don't just practice your slap shot because it's your favorite. Practice all manner of shots. In the game, you may get just one chance. It might be an awkward, off-balance backhander. Prepare for it.

PRO TIPS AND TRICKS

Alex Ovechkin of the Washington Capitals is a brilliant goal scorer. "Nobody ever tells me to give them a pass," says Ovechkin. "My job is to score goals." But it's not Ovechkin's shooting that makes him great. It is his attitude. He is a complete hockey player. "If coach says I must play goalie, I will play goalie," he says. "My weapon isn't my shot. It's me."

Alex Ovechkin

24 PREGAME ATTITUDE

The game is starting in a few minutes. You are warmed up and ready to play—physically. You need to be mentally prepared as well. Hockey is a fast sport with a hard, flying puck. It is easy to fear the puck or your fast-skating opponents. Feeling anxious is normal. If you didn't have some butterflies, it might mean you don't care enough. You just don't want to be gripped by fear, because you cannot play at your best this way. Relax and take a few deep breaths. Imagine making smart passes or playing solid defense. Be confident. You have worked hard in practice, right? Convince yourself that your hard work is about to pay off.

Even the NHL's all-time great players, like Mario Lemieux (pictured here), had to be mentally prepared before the game. Have confidence in your abilities and remember the hard work you put in at practice. Relax and great things will happen.

25 SPORTSMANSHIP

In golf or tennis, the focus is on you. Hockey is a team sport. You are not out there to get all the attention. You want to help your team win. If you score a goal—celebrate! Just remember to thank the teammate who created the shot for you. Praise others for their effort. Never complain about someone failing to make a pass or helping out on defense. Your coach should handle that. After the game, win or lose, show good sportsmanship toward your opponents by shaking hands. The respect you show others will make your hockey experience rewarding.

You cannot succeed without the help of your teammates. Praise your teammates for their efforts and show good sportsmanship to your opponents— win or lose. Play hard and you can celebrate after the game.

DID YOU KNOW?

A pro hockey player loses about five pounds in a game. You probably lose at least half that in yours.

GLOSSARY

body check—To purposely make contact with an opponent. Most hard body checking is not allowed in youth hockey.

check—To defend an opponent closely.

crease—The small, marked half-moon shape in front of the goal, in which only a goalie can be in most circumstances.

crossover—A technique in which you cross your outside skate over your inside skate to skate in a curve.

face-off—A contest between two opponents to gain control of the puck as it is dropped between them by the official.

funneling—Approaching your opponent with the puck at an angle to force him or her toward your teammate or the boards.

glide leg—The leg over which your weight shifts for basic skating. Your glide leg then becomes your push leg.

push leg—The leg that is usually forward in your stance to be used to launch you ahead.

redirect—Change the direction or line of a shot.

screening—Standing in front of your opponent to block his or her sight of the action.

shadowed—Closely guarded, as if your opponent were your shadow.

slot—The area between face-off circles about twenty feet from the goal.

square—In hockey, the position of the stick blade in relation to the target. The blade is square when it is perpendicular, or at a right angle, to the target.

FURTHER READING

Books

Biskup, Agnieszka. *Hockey: How It Works*. Mankato, Minn.: Capstone Press, 2010.

Crossingham, John. *Slap Shot Hockey*. New York: Crabtree Publishing Co., 2008.

Kennedy, Mike, and Mike Stewart. *Score!: The Action and Artistry of Hockey's Magnificent Moment*. Minneapolis, Minn.: Millbrook Press, 2010.

McKinley, Michael. *Ice Time: The Story of Hockey*. Toronto: Tundra Books, 2006.

Thomas, Keltie. *Inside Hockey!: The Legends, Facts, and Feats That Made the Game Great*. Toronto: Maple Tree Press, 2008.

Internet Addresses

Hockey Hall of Fame
<http://www.hhof.com/>

NHL.com: The Learning Center
<http://www.flexxcoach.com/learningcenter/>

The Science of Hockey
<http://www.exploratorium.edu/hockey/>

INDEX